Traveling on the River of Time

Lauren O. Thyme

A do-it-yourself handbook for the exploration of past lives

How to uncover your past and heal your present

Lauren O. Thyme Publishing

Printed in the United States of America

ISBN: 978-0-9983446-4-5

For information contact:

Lauren O. Thyme Publishing
LaurenOThymecreations.com or
thymelauren.wixsite.com/thymely-one
Thyme.lauren@gmail.com

ALSO BY LAUREN O. THYME

The Lemurian Way: Remembering your Essential Nature

Along the Nile

Cosmic Grandma Wisdom

Twin Souls: a Karmic Love Story

Strangers in Paradise

Forgiveness equals Fortune, co-authored with Liah Holtzman

Thymely Tales: Transformational fairy tales for adults and children

From the Depths of Thyme: Poems of Life, Sex, and Transformation

Alternatives for Everyone, a Guide to Non-traditional Health Care

This is dedicated to my beloved Aunt Edna who gave me spiritual and metaphysical books to read beginning when I was 9 years old and always encouraged my abilities and memories.

Disclaimer

This book is not intended to diagnose nor heal any ailments you may be experiencing and thus bears no liability for you reading this book and doing the exercises. I am not a doctor nor a therapist. If in doubt, please see your doctor and/or psychologist before doing any of the techniques.

Contents

WHAT ARE PAST LIVES?

What are past lives? Loosely put, I use the term to describe other earthly experiences one has had in addition to one's current lifetime. Those experiences have occurred in varying epochs, countries, cultures, and races, and includes one's soul experiencing both sexes in other lifetimes.

Do you have to believe in past lives or reincarnation to gain benefit from my method?

No, you don't.

Why is it important to be concerned with past lives? Because unhealed, unexplored past lives, especially difficult ones, can shape your current life, affecting your relationships, health, finances, as well as mental and emotional states.

Time is not linear. All lives, including one's current life, are happening in present time, what Eckhardt Tolle calls the "Now." Although I use the term past lives, all thoughts, actions, behaviors, and feelings are occurring in present time. In fact, according to quantum physicists, string theorists, metaphysicians, and spiritual teachers, time is different than what we have believed and understood.

One's current life can transform and improve when one works on healing problems and issues from those past lives.

Past life traumas from another lifetime can be experienced and released, which then alters and enhances one's current lifetime.

Furthermore, your past lives can/will also change when you work on yourself in your current lifetime identity through conscious activities such as meditation, bodywork, prayer, and positive changes in thought and behavior -- especially forgiveness and compassion. In other words because all lifetimes are operating in the now, lifetimes are fluid and interchangeable, and can be transformed purposefully.

I currently remember 97 lifetimes in detail, the memories starting when I was five years old. When I meet certain people, I can discern which lifetimes I knew them in, what our relationship was like, and what we are still working through together. Ultimately the goal seems to be forgiveness, peace, and balance. Having this knowledge and information helps me work through problems in myself and in relationships.

Long ago I discovered that I am a "battery" for other lifetimes, which accesses information easily and effortlessly, both for me and for others.

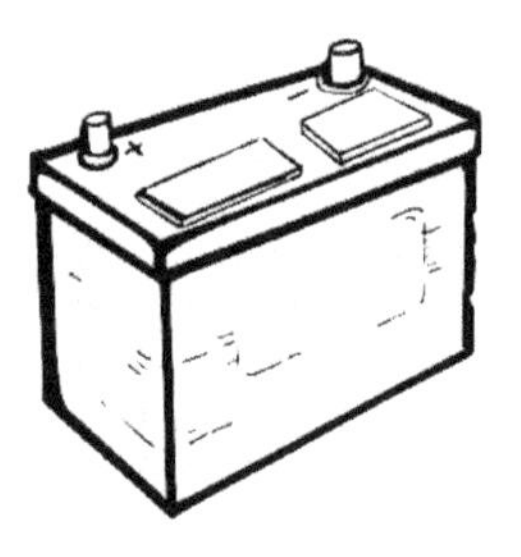

This mysterious juice, the vibrational charge that is connected to me and works through me, helps bring past lives into vivid focus and understanding. The vibrant energy and ease of the battery is captured in this booklet to assist you in your exploration.

After consulting for decades with other individuals on their past lives, an interesting aspect became clear. What is known as karma doesn't get created from what one does or doesn't do in a certain lifetime, but how one THINKS or FEELS about what he/she did or didn't do, as well as how one THINKS or FEELS about other people's actions or lack of action. This often results in guilt, anger, fear, blame, remorse, shame, and revenge in one's current lifetime.

At some point in its evolution the soul makes a decision to reverse or balance those erroneous assumptions, as well as to experience challenging issues relating to key individuals. Many times taking on the issues and deciding to upgrade one's soul results in tackling difficult lessons in one lifetime, analogous to going to a university to learn advanced curriculums. Thus the soul waits for an appropriate lifetime in which to work out a particular problem or problematic relationship.

I've been a practicing astrologer for 45 years. I've concluded that the birth chart is a blueprint for the current life indicating challenges, talents, proclivities, obsessions, relationships, along with personality characteristics and defects. Thus the difficulties you experience are not wrong or bad in your chart. You have chosen obstacles and complications to achieve further knowledge and progress in the school of life.

A soul cannot learn everything in one short lifetime, so the soul chooses a few qualities to play with and learn about each time through hundreds or perhaps thousands of lifetimes.

Therefore, if a person has a problem, the soul has chosen that difficulty to learn and grow spiritually, as well as to heal and balance itself through understanding and compassion for itself and others.

Although a soul may choose to lead a disruptive life, it does not mean that particular lifetime is bad or evil. I don't believe in evil. A soul needs to have numerous experiences in order to grow and learn, which includes what we might consider "good" and "bad."

In my decades of work I notice that nowadays many souls are leading multiple lives in one lifetime – having many significant relationships, moving homes frequently, as well as having various jobs or careers. What I believe is happening is that time is speeding up on planet Earth and there is a lot to accomplish in a short amount of time. Our planet is going through challenging times.

Souls travel through lifetimes in soul groups or soul families. Often a soul friend / family member will either assist another soul to weather a stormy lifetime or to create challenging situations to be worked out together.

There are hundreds of books published on this topic. So ... why did I write this handbook and what are the benefits of your pursuing the exercises?

I offer a method for you to explore your past lives easily and effortlessly, without trauma, without hypnosis, or hiring any person to guide you. Essentially you do this work by yourself for free - except for the minimal cost of the handbook. You can pilot yourself anytime, as often as you like. Your Higher Self and its wisdom will be in charge.

You can think of yourself as a deep sea diver, exploring the vast depths and infinite reaches of your soul's experiences.

You can also assist your friends and relatives on a journey of discovery – or gift them with their own handbooks.

One's experience using this method is what can inform and heal your soul in its journey, to modify or even eliminate your current lifetime problems and expand positive events and attributes.

When you heal past life issues, you heal yourself.

When you heal yourself, you heal your past life issues, which is positive reinforcement for your soul's growth and evolution. That healing continues and expands in an endless spiral of spiritual improvement.

You will find this process simple, restful, and comfortable. You will be at ease throughout the session without upset or trauma. You will feel relaxed, peaceful, yet alert. If you get stuck at any time in the process, you are advised to "make it up." In other words make up a story.

As the mystic, writer, poet, and artist William Blake said,

> "The imagination is not a state: it is the human existence itself."

Imagination is not fantasy or illusions, but our higher consciousness revealing itself to us.

My procedure will help you to release control of the mental, ego-centered, logical mind, and transport you to the perceptive "Higher Self" who will effortlessly divulge accurate information on your behalf in a contemplative, gentle manner.

You do not need to believe in reincarnation or past lives for this method to work. You can consider that what you learn through this technique are symbols and archetypes which describe and illuminate your current life.

PREPARATION

In order to be in a peaceful condition to do this work, allow yourself at least an hour without interruptions in a quiet, calm environment. You can meditate first, take a hot bath, or a nap, to help you unwind, to more easily reach into the inner sanctum of your consciousness, to be guided by your Higher Self.

You can keep a notebook, cellphone or laptop at your side to make notes.

BEGINNING

Decide what you want to learn from your exploration into past lives. For example:

- You can investigate relationships from past lives for someone you know in your current lifetime, such as an enemy, a dear friend, a child, or a lover;
- You may focus on current obstacles and problems, or ill health to uncover tribulations, poor choices, or decisions you have made in past lives;
- You might concentrate on jobs, careers or talents that you've had in the past in order to stimulate ideas on how to formulate a career in your current lifetime. Your lifetimes will probably be ordinary. A soul chooses to be a powerful, historical person only *rarely* in lifetimes. Then that experience is often shared by many other souls.
- I ask that you set aside your logical mind. Imagine that you are putting it on a table next to you. You won't need it for this experience. You will be "making it up" as you go along. You cannot anticipate any exact answer as to what you will see, feel, hear, or sense on your voyage of discovery and you will have no way to prove or disprove what you uncover.
- Logic, rationality, and reasoning will be of no help nor necessary on this expedition. However, what you unearth will make profound sense to you and "feel" correct. Plus you will be creating a valuable tool to gain information and learn how to trust your inner guidance, even if you have never done so before now.
- If you wish, you can close your eyes in order to focus better.

Your Journey
Begins

STARTING ON THE VOYAGE

- Imagine that your soul's vessel is moored on the River of Time.

- Get in and set sail or start the engine. If you like, you can bring with you a trusted friend, guide, counselor, teacher, or sage.
- You can pilot the boat or let someone else do it for you.
- Then begin traveling along the River of Time.
- You will notice scenery around you. Take your time. Relax. You will see piers, docks, harbors, ports, anchorages, wharfs, and moorings.

- Continue to travel along the River until you find a place that interests you. If you are unsure where to stop, that's okay. You are learning to trust your intuition. If you are confused or hesitant, I encourage you to just "make it up."
- "But what if I'm fantasizing?" you may ask. Imagining? Dreaming? Daydreaming? Actually, those are links to your inner world and to your past lives. So encourage yourself. You don't have to know for sure. You don't have to figure it out. Your logic is not important here. Only your experiences and your intuitions have meaning in this quest.
- When you find a mooring on the River of Time that seems interesting or draws your attention, guide your boat there.

- Tie up your boat at the dock, get out, and walk up the pier to your destination.

❋ At the end of the pier is a closed door.

❋ Open the door and walk through, closing it behind you.

WHO IS BEHIND THE DOOR?

- ❋ In front of you is a mirror. Look into it and examine the person that you see reflected there. It is you as you appeared in that lifetime.

✯ Are you male or female?

✯ What race are you?
✯ Old or young?

✯ What color is your hair?
✯ Your eyes?

- How are you dressed? What you are wearing will help in locating the period of time you find yourself in. Are you dressed well or poorly?

- Rags or expensive clothing?

- Your clothing (or lack of clothing) will determine the social/economic milieu you find yourself in and perhaps are a part of.

- Now ask yourself what country are you in? Can you determine this by how you're dressed? If you're unsure, make it up.

- Next to the mirror is a calendar. What is the month, day, and year? If you are undecided, "make it up." A date will pop into your head.
- Ask yourself "what is my age?" If you don't know or can't decide, "make it up." An answer will pop into your head.

THE 1ST IMPORTANT EVENT OF THAT LIFE

Go to the 1st important event of that life -- now.

- How old are you during this event? What are the circumstances of this event?
- Use all your senses to experience it. Feel it, see it, hear, even smell what is happening.
- What are people saying to you?
- Can you hear any sounds?
- Where are you? Are you outside or inside?
- Describe the countryside. What is the weather like?
- Are you near a body of water?
    - Mountains?
    - Pasture?
    - Jungle?
    - Desert?

- In a room of a simple house?

- A castle?

❋ A cave?

❋ Describe it. Feel it. See it. Hear it. Let your senses become acute

❋ Are you with an individual or group? Describe the person or persons to yourself.

❋ Be patient and let the clarity arise of its own accord.

❋ If you are unsure, confused, or don't perceive anything, "make it up."

Don't be worried that you could be wrong or mistaken. Nothing is erroneous or incorrect in this experience. You are learning to trust yourself and to have faith in whatever is revealed for yourself. Let the answers pop into your head.

❋ What does this event mean to you? If you are unsure or don't know, "make it up."

❋ What are your emotions?

- ❋ Did you create any decisions based on this event?

If you find yourself getting upset, take a deep breath, slowly exhale and relax. This method is not meant to bring you pain, rather illumination and release. If you wish, you may detach yourself from any upsetting feelings and simply be an observer.

- ❋ Take a long deep breath and slowly exhale. Relax.

After you have thoroughly examined this experience to your satisfaction, go to the next important event of your life.

THE 2nd IMPORTANT EVENT OF THAT LIFE

Go there now.

- How old are you during this event? What are the circumstances of this event?
- Use all your senses to experience it.
  - Feel it
  - See it
  - Hear what is happening.
- What are people saying to you?
- Are there any scents you can discern?
- Can you hear any sounds?
- Where are you?

- Are you outside or inside?
- What is the weather like?

- Describe the countryside.
- Are you near a body of water?
    - Mountains?
    - Pasture?
    - Jungle?
    - Desert?
- In a room of a house? A castle? A cave? A village?
    - Describe it.
    - Feel it.
    - See it.
    - Hear it.
    - Smell it.
    - Are you with an individual or group?
    - Be patient and let the clarity arise of its own accord.

If you are unsure, confused, or don't perceive anything, "make it up."

Let go of worry that you might be wrong or mistaken. Nothing is erroneous or incorrect in this experience. You are learning to trust yourself and to have faith in whatever comes up for yourself. Answers will simply pop into your head.

- What does this event mean to you? If you are unsure or don't know, "make it up."
  - What are your emotions?
  - Did you make any decisions based on this event?

If you find yourself getting upset, take a deep breath, slowly exhale and relax. This method is not meant to bring you pain, rather illumination and release. You can float above the situation to feel more detached.

- What does this second event mean to you? If you are unsure or don't know, "make it up."
- Is this event connected in any way to the first event?
- Take your time to soak in all the details of this event.
- Take a long slow breath in and slowly exhale. Relax.

After you have thoroughly investigated this 2nd experience to your satisfaction, go to the next important (3rd) event.

THE 3rd IMPORTANT EVENT OF THAT LIFE

Go there now.

- ❋ How old are you during this event?

What are the circumstances of this event?

- ❋ Use all your senses to experience it.

    - ✯ Feel it,
    - ✯ see it,
    - ✯ hear what is happening.

- ❋ What are people saying to you?

- ❋ Are there any scents you can discern?

- ❋ Can you hear any sounds?

- Where are you?
    - Are you outside or inside?
    - What is the weather like?
    - Describe the countryside.

- Are you near a body of water?
- Mountains?
- Pasture?
- Desert?
- Jungle?

- In a room of a house or other building? A castle? A cave? A hut?
- Describe it. Feel it. See it. Hear it.

- Are you with an individual or group? Describe the person or group to yourself.
- What is the action you observe? Are you part of it?
- Be patient and let the clarity arise of its own accord.
- If you are unsure, confused, or don't perceive anything, "make it up."

Don't be worried that you could be wrong or mistaken. Nothing is erroneous or incorrect in this experience. You are learning to trust yourself and to have faith in whatever comes up for yourself. Answers will simply pop into your head. Trust them.

- What does this event mean to you? If you are unsure or don't know, "make it up."
- What are your emotions?
- Did you make any decisions based on this event?

If you find yourself getting upset, take a deep breath, exhale slowly and relax. This method is not meant to bring you pain, rather illumination and release. You can float above the situation to feel more detached.

What do these 3 events mean to you? Is this 3rd event connected in any important way to the other events? Do they fit together? In what way? If you are unsure or don't know, "make it up."

- Is this event or lifetime connected to the people you know today in your current lifetime? Describe.
- Take your time to soak in all the details of this event.
- After you have thoroughly investigated this 3rd experience to your satisfaction, take a slow, deep breath and exhale. Relax.

THE MOMENT BEFORE DEATH IN THAT LIFE

Move to the moment just before your death in that lifetime.

Be there now.

- ❋ How old are you?
- ❋ What is your physical condition?

- ❋ How did you get to that condition?
- ❋ Are one or more people with you?
    - ✯ Who are they?
    - ✯ What did they mean to you?
    - ✯ If no one is there with you, why not?
    - ✯ Are there people with you that you recognize from your current lifetime?
- ❋ How did your life change before your death?
    - ✯ Better? or Worse?

- What do you think about your life as you look at these events?
    - Any emotions?
    - Regrets?
    - Resolutions?
    - Decisions?

Take a slow, deep breath and let it out. Relax.

RELEASING THAT LIFE TO YOUR HIGHER SELF

Now relax and let yourself slide out of your physical body as you sense your body dying. Feel the release and peace as you do so

- As you rise towards the sky, imagine a brilliant white/gold luminescence above you. Waiting there for you is your Higher Self who is a bright light, filled with love. You feel joy and relief at seeing your Higher Self and the Higher Self is joyful to be with you as well.
- You merge with the Higher Self effortlessly and you feel the delight and ecstasy of that reunion.
- As you do so, you turn your attention towards the body and the life you have just exited. You now have infinite knowledge and wisdom to understand that life. You can receive messages from within you and your Higher Self. If you get stuck, make up an answer.
- What did you finish in that life?
- Did you leave anything undone?
- Did you accomplish what you had set out to do?
- Did you meet the souls you intended to meet?
- Is there any grief remaining in the body and life you have just departed? Remorse? Bitterness? Anger? Sadness?
- What other emotions did you have upon dying?
- Did you make any decisions as what you want to do in the future for further learning, growth and evolution and to balance the scales of that life?
- Do you recognize any of the people you knew in that life as being in your current life? If so, who are they in your present lifetime? What is the type and quality of your

relationship with each person that you knew while in that other lifetime?

- As you assimilate all this information, take a deep breath and liberate the knowledge. Breathe out all your emotions and decisions and let them depart. Watch them rise like weightless hot air balloons up into the gold/white light above you where they dissolve easily and gently, evaporating into nothingness.

- Thank yourself for receiving the knowledge of the lifetime you have just observed.
- Allow forgiveness and gratitude for who you were and what you learned flood into your awareness.
- Thank all the people who participated in that life with you, no matter how easy or difficult each relationship had been.
- Take a deep breath and slowly exhale. Relax.

Take In This Life!

If you are willing and have enough time and energy, you may take another journey of discovery to a different lifetime.

If you prefer not to continue, at this time, go to Page 79 RETURNING HOME

EXPLORING 2ND LIFETIME

If you are willing and have enough time and energy, you may take another journey of discovery to a different lifetime.

- Exit through the door you first entered, get back into the boat, release it from its mooring, and begin once again to travel along the River of Time.

- When you find a mooring on the River of Time that seems interesting or draws your attention, guide your boat there. Fasten your boat at the dock, get out, and walk up the pier to your destination.
- At the end of the pier is a closed door. Open the door and walk in, closing it behind you.

Now you will repeat the steps you took in the first lifetime you examined.

❋ In front of you is a mirror.

❋ Look into it and examine the person you see in the mirror. That person was you in that other lifetime

- ✯ Are you male or female?
- ✯ Old or young?
- ✯ What race are you?
- ✯ What color is your hair?
- ✯ Your eyes?
- ✯ How are you dressed?

- What you are wearing will help in locating the period of time you find yourself in.
    - Are you dressed well or poorly?
    - Rags or expensive clothing?
    - Your clothing (or lack of clothing) will determine the social/economic milieu you find yourself in and perhaps are a part of.
    - Ask yourself what country are you in? Can you determine this by how you're dressed? If you're unsure, make it up.

- Next to the mirror is a calendar. What is the month, day, and year? If you are undecided, "make it up." A date will pop into your mind.
- Ask yourself "what is my age?" If you don't know or can't decide, "make it up." An age will pop into your mind.

FIRST IMPORTANT EVENT OF 2ND LIFE

- Now go to the first important event of that life.
- How old are you during this event?
- What are the circumstances of this event?
- Use all your senses to experience it.
    - Feel it, see it, hear what is happening.
- What are people saying to you?
- Are there any scents you can discern?
- Can you hear any sounds?
- Where are you? Are you outside or inside? What is the weather like?
- Describe the countryside.
    - Are you near a body of water?
    - Mountains?
    - Pasture?
    - Jungle?
    - Desert?
- In a room of a house or other building? A castle? A cave?
    - Describe it.
    - Feel it.
    - See it.
    - Hear it.

- Are you with an individual or group?

Be patient and let the clarity arise of its own accord. If you are unsure, confused, or don't perceive anything, "make it up." Don't be worried that you could be wrong or mistaken. Nothing is erroneous or incorrect in this experience. You are learning to trust yourself and to have faith in whatever comes up for yourself

- What does this event mean to you? If you are unsure or don't know, "make it up."
- What are your emotions?
- Did you create any decisions based on this event?

If you find yourself getting upset, take a deep breath, exhale slowly and relax. This method is not meant to bring you pain, rather illumination and release. If you wish, you may detach yourself from any upsetting feelings and be an observer.

Take another long deep breath and slowly exhale.

After you have thoroughly investigated that event to your satisfaction, go to the next important event of your life.

SECOND IMPORTANT EVENT OF 2ND LIFE

Go there now.

- How old are you during this event? What are the circumstances of this event?
- Use all your senses to experience it. Feel it, see it, hear what is happening.
- What are people saying to you?
- Are there any scents you can discern?
- Can you hear any sounds?
- Where are you?
  - Are you outside or inside?
  - What is the weather like?
  - Describe the countryside.
- Are you near a body of water?
  - Mountains?
  - Pasture?
- In a room of a house? A castle? A cave?
  - Describe it.
  - Feel it.
  - See it.
  - Hear it.
  - Smell it.
- Are you with an individual or group?

Be patient and let the clarity arise of its own accord. If you are unsure, confused, or don't perceive anything, "make it up."

Don't be worried that you could be wrong or mistaken. Nothing is erroneous or incorrect in this experience. You are learning to trust yourself and to have faith in whatever comes up for yourself.

What does this event mean to you? If you are unsure or don't know, "make it up."

What are your emotions?

If you find yourself getting upset, take a deep breath, exhale slowly and relax. This method is not meant to bring you pain, rather illumination and release. You can float above the situation to feel more detached.

- What does this second event mean to you? If you are unsure or don't know, "make it up."
- Did you make any decisions based on this event?
- Is this event connected in any way to the first event?
- Take your time to soak in all the details of this event.
- Take a long slow breath in and slowly exhale. Relax.

After you have thoroughly investigated this second experience to your satisfaction, go to the next important (3rd) event.

THIRD IMPORTANT EVENT OF 2ND LIFE

Go there now.

- How old are you during this event?
- What are the circumstances of this event?

- Use all your senses to experience it. Feel it, see it, hear what is happening.
- What are people saying to you?
- Are there any scents you can discern?
- Can you hear any sounds?
- Where are you?
- Are you outside or inside?
- What is the weather like?
- Describe the countryside.
- Are you near a body of water? Mountains? Pasture?

- In a room of a house? A castle? A cave?
    - Describe it.
    - Feel it.
    - See it.
    - Hear it.
- Are you with an individual or group?
- What is the action you observe? Are you part of it?

Be patient and let the clarity arise of its own accord. If you are unsure, confused, or don't perceive anything, "make it up." Don't be worried that you could be wrong or mistaken. Nothing is erroneous or incorrect in this experience. You are learning to trust yourself and to have faith in whatever comes up for yourself.

- What does this event mean to you? If you are unsure or don't know, "make it up."
- What are your emotions?
- Did you create any decisions based on this event?

If you find yourself getting upset, take a deep breath, exhale slowly and relax. This method is not meant to bring you pain, rather illumination and release. You can float above the situation to feel more detached.

- What do these 3 events mean to you? How do they fit together?
- If you are unsure or don't know, "make it up."
- What are your emotions?
- Did you make any decisions based on this event?
- Is this event connected in any way to the first or second events?
- Take your time to soak in all the details of this event.

- What does this third event mean to you? If you are unsure or don't know, "make it up."
- Did you make any decisions based on these 3 events? Is this event connected in an important way to the first or second event?
- Is this event connected to the people you know today?
- Take your time to soak in all the details of this event.

THE MOMENT BEFORE DEATH IN 2ND LIFE

After you have thoroughly investigated the 3rd experience to your satisfaction, take a slow, deep breath, let it out and relax. Now you will move to the moment just before your death in that lifetime.

- How old are you?

- What is your physical condition?
- How did you get to that condition?
- Are one or more people with you?
    - Who are they?
    - What did they mean to you?
    - Are they people you know today in your current lifetime?
    - If no one is there, why not?
- How did your life change before your death? Better? Worse?

- What do you think about your life as you look at these events?
- Emotions?
- Regrets?
- Resolutions?
- Decisions?

RELEASING THAT LIFE TO YOUR HIGHER SELF 2ND LIFE

Take a slow, deep breath and exhale.

- Now relax and let yourself slide out of your physical body as you sense your body dying. Feel the release and peace as you do so.
- As you rise towards the sky, imagine a brilliant white/gold light above you. Waiting there for you is your Higher Self who is a bright light, filled with love. You feel joy and relief at seeing your Higher Self and the Higher Self is happy in seeing you as well.
- You merge into that self effortlessly and you feel the delight and ecstasy of that reunion.
- As you do so, you turn your attention towards the body and the life you have just exited. You now have infinite knowledge and wisdom to understand that life. You can receive messages from within you / Higher Self.
- What did you finish in that life?
- Did you leave anything undone?
- Did you accomplish what you had set out to do?
- Did you meet the souls you intended to meet?
- Is there any grief remaining in that body and the life you have just left? Remorse? Bitterness? Anger? Sadness?
- What other emotions did you have upon dying?
- Did you make any decisions as what you want to do in the future for further learning, growth and evolution and to balance the scales of that life?
- Do you recognize any of the people you knew in that life as being in your current life? If so, who are they in your

present lifetime? What is the quality of your relationship with each person that you knew while there?

- As you assimilate all this information, take a deep breath and liberate the knowledge.

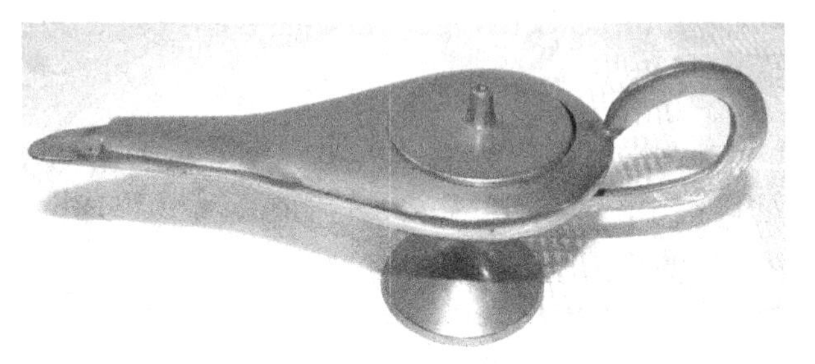

- Let all your emotions and decisions depart. Watch those rise up into the gold/white light above you and dissolve easily and gently, evaporating into light.
- Thank yourself for receiving the knowledge of this lifetime you have observed and allow forgiveness and gratitude for who you were flood into your awareness.
- Thank each person who participated in that life with you, no matter how easy or difficult each relationship had been.
- Take a deep breath and slowly exhale. Relax.

If you are willing and have enough time and energy, you may take a final journey of discovery to a third lifetime. I have found that working through 3 lifetimes in one session is enough for one session. You can come back to this method any time you desire.

Take In This Life!

If you are willing and have enough time and energy, you may take another journey of discovery to a different lifetime.

If you prefer not to continue, at this time, go to Page 79 RETURNING HOME

EXPLORING 3rd LIFETIME

❋Exit through the door you first entered, get back into the boat, release it from its mooring, and once again begin to travel along the River of Time.

❋When you find a mooring on the River of Time that seems interesting or draws your attention, guide your boat there. Fasten your boat at the dock, get out, and walk up the pier to your destination.

❋ At the end of the pier is a closed door. Open the door and walk in, closing it behind you. Now you will repeat the steps you took in the first lifetime you examined.

❋ In front of you will see a mirror. Look into it and examine the person who you see in the mirror. That is you in the lifetime you just entered.

- ✯ Are you male or female?
- ✯ Old or young?
- ✯ What race are you?
- ✯ What color is your hair?
- ✯ Your eyes?

- How are you dressed?
- What you are wearing will help in locating the period of time you find yourself in.
- Are you dressed well or poorly?
- Rags or expensive clothing? Your clothing (or lack of clothing) will determine the social/economic milieu you find yourself in and perhaps are a part of.

- Ask yourself what country are you in? Can you determine this by how you're dressed? If you're unsure, make it up.
- Ask yourself "what is my age?" If you don't know or can't decide, "make it up." An answer will pop into your head. Trust it.
- Next to the mirror is a calendar. What is the month, day, and year? If you are undecided, "make it up." An answer will pop into your head. Trust it.

FIRST IMPORTANT EVENT OF 3RD LIFE

Go there now.

- How old are you during this event? What are the circumstances of this event?
- Use all your senses to experience it. Feel it, see it, hear what is happening.
- What are people saying to you?
- Are there any scents you can discern?
- Can you hear any sounds?
- Where are you?
  - Are you outside or inside?
  - What is the weather like?
  - Describe the countryside.

- Are you near a body of water? Mountains? Pasture? Desert? Jungle?

- Are you in a room of a house or other building? A castle? A cave? A hut?
- Describe it. Feel it. See it. Hear it.
- Are you with an individual or group?
- Be patient and let the clarity arise of its own accord.
- If you are unsure, confused, or don't perceive anything, "make it up." Don't be worried that you could be wrong or mistaken.
- Nothing is erroneous or incorrect in this experience.
- You are learning to trust yourself and to have faith in whatever comes up for yourself.
- What does this event mean to you? If you are unsure or don't know, "make it up."
- What are your emotions?
- Did you formulate any decisions based on this event?
- If you find yourself getting upset, take a deep breath, exhale slowly and relax. This method is not meant to bring you pain, rather illumination and release. If you wish, you may detach yourself from any upsetting feelings and be an observer.
- Take another long deep breath and slowly exhale.
- After you have thoroughly investigated this experience to your satisfaction, go to the next important event of your life.

SECOND IMPORTANT EVENT OF 3RD LIFE

Go there now.

- ❋ How old are you during this event? What are the circumstances of this event?
- ❋ Use all your senses to experience it. Feel it, see it, hear what is happening.
- ❋ What are people saying to you?
- ❋ Are there any scents you can discern?
- ❋ Can you hear any sounds?
- ❋ Where are you?
    - ✯ Are you outside or inside?
    - ✯ What is the weather like?
    - ✯ Describe the countryside.

- ❋ Are you near a body of water? Mountains? Pasture? Jungle? Desert?
- ❋ In a room of a house or other building? A castle? A cave? A church?
    - ✯ Describe it.
    - ✯ Feel it.
    - ✯ See it.
    - ✯ Hear it.
    - ✯ Smell it.

- Are you with an individual or group?
- Be patient and let the clarity arise of its own accord. If you are unsure, confused, or don't perceive anything, "make it up." Don't be worried that you could be wrong or mistaken.
- Nothing is erroneous or incorrect in this experience.
- You are learning to trust yourself and to have faith in whatever comes up for yourself.

- What does this event mean to you? If you are unsure or don't know, "make it up."
- What are your emotions?
- Did you create any decisions based on this event?
- If you find yourself getting upset, take a deep breath, exhale slowly and relax. This method is not meant to bring you pain, rather illumination and release.
- You can float above the situation to feel more detached.
- What does this second event mean to you? If you are unsure or don't know, "make it up."

- What are your emotions?
- Did you make any decisions based on this event?
- Is this event connected in any way to the first event?
- Take your time to soak in all the details of this event.
- Take a long slow breath in and slowly exhale. Relax.

After you have thoroughly investigated this experience to your satisfaction, go to the next important (3rd) event.

THIRD IMPORTANT EVENT OF 3rd LIFE

Go there now.

- How old are you during this event? What are the circumstances of this event?
- Use all your senses to experience it. Feel it, see it, hear what is happening.
- What are people saying to you?
- Are there any scents you can discern?
- Can you hear any sounds?
- Where are you? Are you outside or inside? What is the weather like? Describe the countryside.
- Are you near a body of water? Mountains? Pasture?
- In a room of a house? A castle? A cave?
    - Describe it.
    - Feel it.
    - See it.
    - Hear it.
- Are you with an individual or group?
- What is the action you observe? Are you part of it?

- Be patient and let the clarity arise of its own accord.

If you are unsure, confused, or don't perceive anything, "make it up." Don't be worried that you could be wrong or mistaken. Nothing is erroneous or incorrect in this experience. You are learning to trust yourself and to have faith in whatever comes up for yourself.

- What does this event mean to you? If you are unsure or don't know, "make it up."
- Is this event connected in any way to the first or second events?
- What do all these events mean to you? How do they fit together?
- If you are unsure or don't know, "make it up."

- What are your emotions?
- Did you make any decisions based on this event?

- If you find yourself getting upset, take a deep breath, exhale slowly and relax. This method is not meant to bring you pain, rather illumination and release.
- You can float above the situation to feel more detached.
- Take your time to soak in all the details of this event.
- What are your emotions?
- Is this event connected in an important way to the people you know today?
- Take your time to digest all the details of this event.

After you have thoroughly investigated this 3rd experience to your satisfaction, take a slow, deep breath and slowly let it out and relax. Now you will move to the moment just before death in that lifetime.

THE MOMENT BEFORE DEATH IN 3RD LIFE

Go there now.

- ❋ How old are you?
- ❋ What is your physical condition?

- ❋ How did you get to that condition?
- ❋ Are one or more people with you? Who are they? What did they mean to you? Are they people you know today in your current lifetime? If no one is there, why not?
- ❋ How did your life change before your death? Better? Worse?
- ❋ What do you think about your life as you look at these events? Emotions? Regrets? Resolutions? Decisions?

Take a slow, deep breath and exhale. Relax.

RELEASING THAT LIFE TO YOUR HIGHER SELF 3RD LIFE

- Now relax and allow yourself to slide out of your physical body as you sense your body dying. Feel the release and peace as you do so.
- As you rise towards the sky, imagine a brilliant white/gold light above you.

Waiting there for you is your Higher Self who is a bright light, filled with love. You feel joy and relief at seeing your Higher Self and the Higher Self is joyful at being with you as well.

- You merge into that Higher Self effortlessly and you feel the delight and ecstasy of that reunion.
- As you do so, you turn your attention towards the body and the life you have just exited. You now have infinite knowledge and wisdom to understand that life. You can receive messages from within you / Higher Self.
- What did you finish in that life?
- Did you leave anything undone?
- Did you accomplish what you had set out to do?
- Did you meet the souls you intended to meet?
- Is there any grief remaining in that body and the life you have just left? Remorse? Bitterness? Anger? Sadness?
- What other emotions did you have upon dying?

- Did you make any decisions as what you want to do in the future for further learning, growth and evolution and to balance the scales of that life?
- Do you recognize any of the people from your current life? If so, who are they in your present lifetime? What are the qualities of your relationships in your current life with those people?
- Take a deep breath and liberate the knowledge. Let all your emotions and decisions leave. Watch them rise like balloons up into the gold/white light above you and dissolve easily and gently.

- Thank yourself for receiving the knowledge of this lifetime you have observed and allow forgiveness and gratitude for who you were flood into your awareness.
- Thank each person who participated in that life with you, no matter how easy or difficult each relationship had been.
- Take a deep breath and slowly exhale. Relax.

Take In This Life!

RETURNING HOME

- Exit through the door you just entered, get back into the boat, release it from its mooring, and return home along the River of Time.

- When you return, get out of the boat. You're back in present time.
- Take a deep breath and slowly exhale. Stretch your arms.
- Feel your feet on the ground.
- Feel the chair beneath you.
- Open your eyes and look around.
- Realize that you have taken an extraordinary journey in search of yourself.

Progressively the lifetimes and events you uncovered and experienced will help in therapeutic changes to your current self, relationships, health, finances, and attitude.

You can return to this method again and again, to learn, recover, heal, and awaken more fully into the pleasure and knowledge of who you are in this lifetime.

Congratulations!

Lauren O. Thyme

NOTES AND ACKNOWLEDGMENTS

My deepest gratitude to Steph Lucas who is brilliant, hard-working, and tireless. Thank you for your help in editing, formatting, publishing, and coming up with great ideas for my books. I am indebted to you always.

Here are some well-known authors who investigated past lives and in-between lives. My deepest appreciation to them and all the other explorers in this psychic realm for their courage and determination to fling open the doors of knowledge for the rest of us.

Edgar Cayce

Brian L. Weiss

Dr. Bruce Goldberg

Sylvia Browne

Manly P. Hall

Dick Sutphen

Helen Wambaugh

Hans Holzer

Robert Schwartz

Dr. Michael Newton

Richard Martini is an award-winning American author, film director, producer, screenwriter and freelance journalist. His latest film Flipside: A Journey into the Afterlife discusses the idea of time in past lifetimes in detail and includes interviews with Dr. Michael Newton and other practitioners from The Newton Institute working with clients.

Richard Martini

"Dr. Michael Newton's first book, Journey of Souls, written in 1994 about *Life Between Lives*, or LBL, the development work was laborious and consumed more than a decade. On this he said, "The research was painfully slow, but as the body of my cases grew [7,000 patients] I finally had a working model of the eternal world where our souls live. After another decade of continuing work and careful research, Dr. Newton published a second book, *Destiny of Souls*, in which he expanded on topics introduced in his first book. In the early 2000's he published another book, *Life Between Lives*, describing his methodology for taking a client into the spirit world for spiritual guidance and illumination. Following this, in an effort to advance the study and practice of his life's work, in 2002, Dr. Newton founded the Society for Spiritual Regression, which evolved into The Newton Institute (TNI) in 2005. The purpose of providing this information about the work and evolving knowledge base about LBL is to illustrate that it came into being after years and years of practice and painstaking, careful research."

http://newtoninstitute.org/news/important-news-michael/

IMAGES AND ILLUSTRATION ATTRIBUTION

We would like to acknowledge and thank the following Graphic Websites for their high quality images.

Pixabay - https://pixabay.com/ - Public Domain under Creative Commons CC0:

Cover
Border
Page 8
Page 9
Page 11
Page 13
Page 17-18
Page 21-23
Page 25-30
Page 33-40
Page 44-58
Page 61-74
Page 79

Designed by Freepik: http://www.freepik.com/

Page 7
Page 16
Page 19
Page 24
Page 41
Page 43
Page 59
Page 75-77

Dreamtime - https://www.dreamstime.com/free-photos - the Creative Commons Zero (CC0) public domain license

Page 17 - BOAT EIGHT dreamstime_xxl_86690039
Page 17 & 79 - BOAT SEVEN dreamstime_xxl_83067943
Page 23 - India lady dreamstime_xxl_82954382
Page 26 - CASTLE dreamstime_xxl_82978330
Page 27 - CAVEdreamstime_xxl_83061451
Page 34 - PYRAMID dreamstime_xxl_83018344
Page 40 - BALLOONS dreamstime_xxl_82948852
Page 45 - PIRATE dreamstimefree_1763788 mario lopes

Made in the USA
Las Vegas, NV
28 August 2021